Victoria

HANNAH & HICKORY

by
Stephen Cosgrove
illustrated by
Wendy Edelson

MULTNOMAH

Other books in this series
Fiddler
Shadow Chaser
Gossamer
Derby Downs
T.J.Flopp
Ira Wordworthy
Persimmony

HANNAH AND HICKORY
© 1990 by Stephen Cosgrove
Published by Multnomah
Portland, Oregon 97266

Printed in the United States

Library of Congress Cataloging-in-Publication-Data

Cosgrove, Stephen.
   Hannah and Hickory / by Stephen Cosgrove ; illustrated by Wendy Edelson.
      p.   cm.
      Summary: The school bully plans to discredit two new students who falsely
   claim to be rich, until he faces his own delusions of grandeur.
      ISBN 0-88070-283-4
      [1. Animals—Fiction. 2. Conduct of life—Fiction.] I. Edelson, Wendy, ill.
   II. Title.
   PZ7.C8187Han   1990
   [E]—dc20
                                                        90-6695
                                                          CIP
                                                          AC

91 92 93 94 95 96 97 98 - 10 9 8 7 6 5 4 3 2

Dedicated to Shaerie and all her memories of childhood.
Through her I learned that home is where the heart is, in the Land of Barely There.

Stephen

arther than far and to the very edge of the horizon was a path bordered in lacy fern. If you walked down that path following the clouds that scuttle across the sky, you would find the land of Barely There.

Barely There . . . a land where the birds reel on wing above the weaver willow trees and warble their happy songs. A land where owls stay awake during the day to tell all who will listen about the delights of this wondrous land . . . Barely There.

If you followed the clouds on their lazy journey, you would come to a place where they misted into rainbow spray. Here you would find a school yard filled with the ringing laughter of children. It was in this old-fashioned schoolhouse that all the creatures from Barely There came when they were young to learn those things that must be learned.

The rusted bell clanged in the much-painted tower of the school. The children giggled and pushed their way up the creaking steps and returned to the sometimes tedious world of books and blackboards.

As the teacher, dear Miss Felicia Fuzzybottom, called the roll to see who was here and who was not, there came up the dusty road a family of four gypsy cats—a mother, a father, and two children. They were dressed in their finest, which, although clean and neat, was old and tattered. Gay, ragged patches of velvet and silk were sewn on knees of both parent and child alike.

The children held back a step or two from their parents as if a little reluctant of the new adventure to come. They clutched in their hands wrinkled bags filled with good things to eat, pencil and paper and ruler too!

This was the Heart family who were newly moved to Barely There and had come to school for the very first time.

Eyes peeked and peered from the schoolroom windows as the Hearts walked up the road.

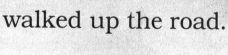

With a clump of boots on well-worn steps and a screech of over-painted hinges, the Hearts came into school with heads held high. Miss Fuzzybottom rushed to welcome all, and the Heart children were introduced to the class, a little too loudly it seemed to them.

"This is my oldest son Hickory and his younger sister Hannah," proudly proclaimed Father Heart. "We are newly moved here and the children must learn what they can, while they can."

Chairs squeaked and necks stretched as everyone checked out the new arrivals. Satisfied that all was well, Father and Mother Heart left the children in the custody and care of the school in Barely There.

Now this school, like other schools, had a rich kid, a big kid, and a bully. In this case, they were all rolled up into one rich, big bully named Bubba—a burly, furry groundhog of monstrous proportions.

As the school bell clanged for recess, he took his group, which was most of the children in the school, to the far side of the playground. There they sat or sprawled upon the ground watching silently as

Hannah and Hickory walked about scuffing dirt on old but well-shined shoes.

No one laughed and no one talked. They all sat silently still, waiting for someone to make the first move. Finally, as was his wont, Bubba called out, "Hey, you! Yeah, *you*, the new kids. Come here!"

Shyly first, and then more boldly, the Heart children moved towards the group.

When they had moved to the edge of the tightly knitted group Bubba asked, "So, why did you guys move here?"

"Well," began Hannah shyly, "we are very poor . . ."

"Poor-ositive!" interrupted Hickory as he pushed his sister aside. "Positive that this is the perfect place to live."

"Hmm," grunted Bubba as he continued his grilling. "So where do you live?"

Once again Hannah started to answer and was interrupted by her brother. "Well," he gushed, "we are very, very rich and we live in a marvelous mansion just over there." Hickory waved his arm vaguely.

"Rich, huh?" pressed Bubba as he squinted his eyes skeptically. "If you are so rich, how come you're wearing ragged clothes with patches?"

"What? These old things?" laughed Hickory. "We wear old clothes whenever we go to a new school so the other kids won't feel bad that they aren't as rich as we are."

All the children clustered about the Hearts as Hickory babbled on about this and that. Bubba, having lost the first round, moved off to the side with the Crony brothers and watched with arched brow.

"I don't like rich snobs," snorted Bubba as he threw himself down on the grass.

"But Bubba," one of the Crony brothers crowed, "you always said that you were rich."

"Yeah," mused Bubba, as he clasped his hands behind his head and watched as Hickory babbled on and on. "I am rich, and I live in a mansion too! But I am me and they are them, and that's a big difference."

With that he didn't wait for the school bell to ring, but went back into the schoolhouse nearly five minutes early.

Bubba brooded the rest of the day as the Hearts became the center of attention. It seemed Miss Fuzzybottom called on one of them every time they raised a hand, and she called on Bubba only once—the only time he didn't know the answer.

Bubba was mad, and Bubba didn't like to get mad. Bubba liked to get even. "Hmmm, I think it's time for a little revenge!" With that he scrawled this note on a bit of lined paper:

Fellow students:

After the final bell has rung, meet me beside the weaver willow. It's time we all welcomed the Hearts to the land of Barely There. Don't say a word. Pass it on!

Bubba

He carefully slipped the note to one of the Cronys and it began its ragged journey around the room, but not to Hickory or Hannah.

Later that day when school was out, all the children met at the weaver willow tree and gathered around Bubba. All, that is, except for Hannah and Hickory, who walked away on the dusty road.

"Let's all follow the 'great' Hannah and Hickory to their palatial castle in the woods," railed Bubba. There we can paint some words of welcome on their castle walls." With that he held up the paint and brushes he had hidden behind his back.

Now, it must be noted that some of the kids didn't want to go, and they left the school grounds straightaway. But the bulk of Bubba's gang thought it was a great idea, and they set off in pursuit of Hannah and Hickory.

As the Heart children walked home, Bubba and the other children followed behind excitedly. With paint and brush in hand they slipped from bush to bush, stopping only when they needed to stifle a giggle.

They continued to shadow behind even as
Hannah and Hickory left the main road to walk down
an old, well-worn path.

The path twisted and turned, and the group had to scurry to keep well hidden. Hannah and Hickory disappeared from view as the path rose and then dropped over a hill. The gang regrouped and Bubba ordered one of the Crony brothers to peek to see when it was safe to follow.

It was but a moment later when the Crony returned, smiling ear to ear. "Hey, guess what, Bubba?" he squealed in delight. "The Hearts don't live in some great palace, they live in Humble Hollow."

"Shanty town!" another cried, "Where all the poor people live."

"Come on, let's all look," yet another laughed.

As one, they crept up the hill and peeked into the valley below.

There, sure enough, was Humble Hollow
with its tumbledown shacks of cardboard and
sticks, and even a tent or two.

"Come on!" shouted the Crony brothers.
"This is even better than a castle. Let's paint
signs all over the shacks to let Hannah and
Hickory know that . . ."

". . . we know!" everyone else shouted. Everyone, except Bubba, who stood apart from the gang.

"Hey, Bubba, let's go get even with the Hearts!" they jeered. But their leader didn't say a word.

Softly but firmly Bubba spoke. "No! You will all go from here and never tell anybody what you saw. Anyone, and I do mean *anyone*, who says anything or even giggles at Hannah or Hickory will have me to deal with, and I think you all know what that means!"

"But they lied, Bubba. They said they were rich and they aren't. They deserve to be humbled," one of the Cronys whined.

"They deserve," growled Bubba, "a little understanding." And then the great bully did something he had never done before . . . he spoke the truth. "Uh, well, . . . I'm not rich either. I don't live in a big mansion. I live in Humble Hollow too."

The other children just stared at Bubba in amazement. Oh, he was still big and burly, but he didn't quite seem the bully anymore. Quietly his fuzzy little friends walked away after vowing not to say a word.

Bubba stood there alone in the waning light of day and looked down on Humble Hollow. Humble Hollow, where weak trails of chimney smoke, starved for more wood, wove ghostly lines against the tattered pines.

He sighed deeply, and then, with a lighter heart, he went down the hill to greet his new neighbors, Hannah and Hickory . . .
in the Land of Barely There.